www.mascotbooks.com

Native American A B C

©2017 Lisa and Colten Lechowicz. All Rights Reserved. No part of this publication may be reproduced, stored in a retrieval system or transmitted in any form by any means electronic, mechanical, or photocopying, recording or otherwise without the permission of the author.

For more information, please contact:
Mascot Books
560 Herndon Parkway #120
Herndon, VA 20170
info@mascotbooks.com

Library of Congress Control Number:2017908348

CPSIA Code: PRT0917A
ISBN-13: 978-1-63177-492-8

Printed in the United States

Native American A B C

by Lisa and Colten Lechowicz

illustrated by Wade Patton

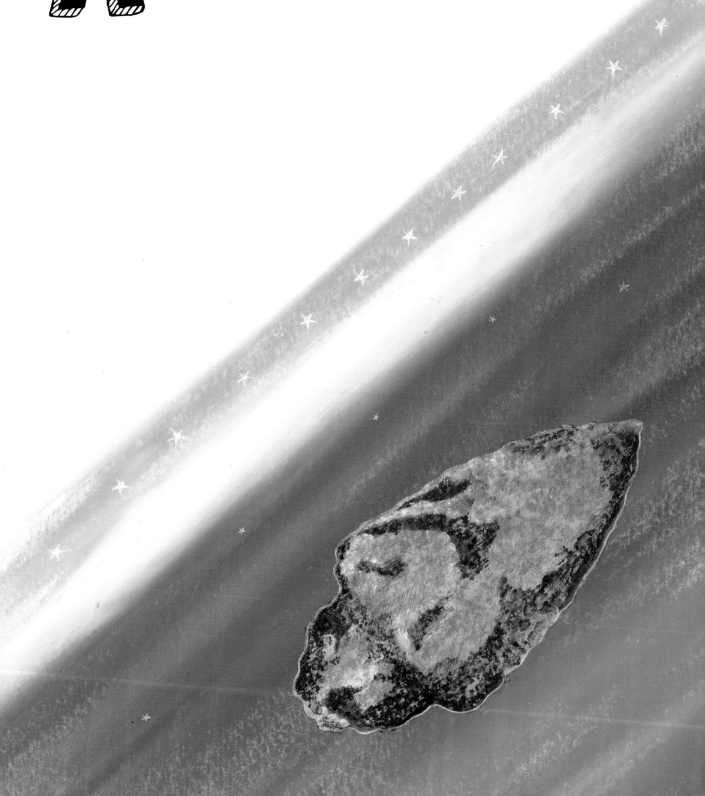

A is for Arrowhead.

The tip of an arrow—sometimes sharp, sometimes blunt.

It is used as a tool or out on the hunt.

 **is for Buffalo.**

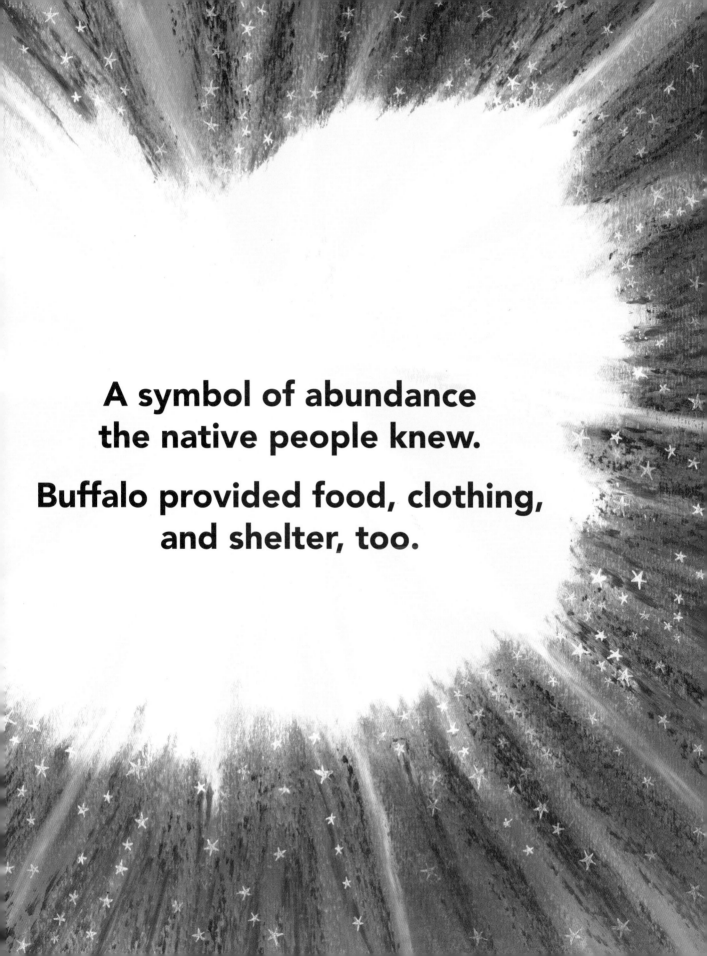

A symbol of abundance
the native people knew.

Buffalo provided food, clothing,
and shelter, too.

C is for Corn.

One of three sisters along
with squash and bean.

At almost every meal,
some form of it was seen.

 **is for Drum.**

An important part of ceremonies, drums are used to call

On spirits and the creator for reasons big and small.

 is for Eagle.

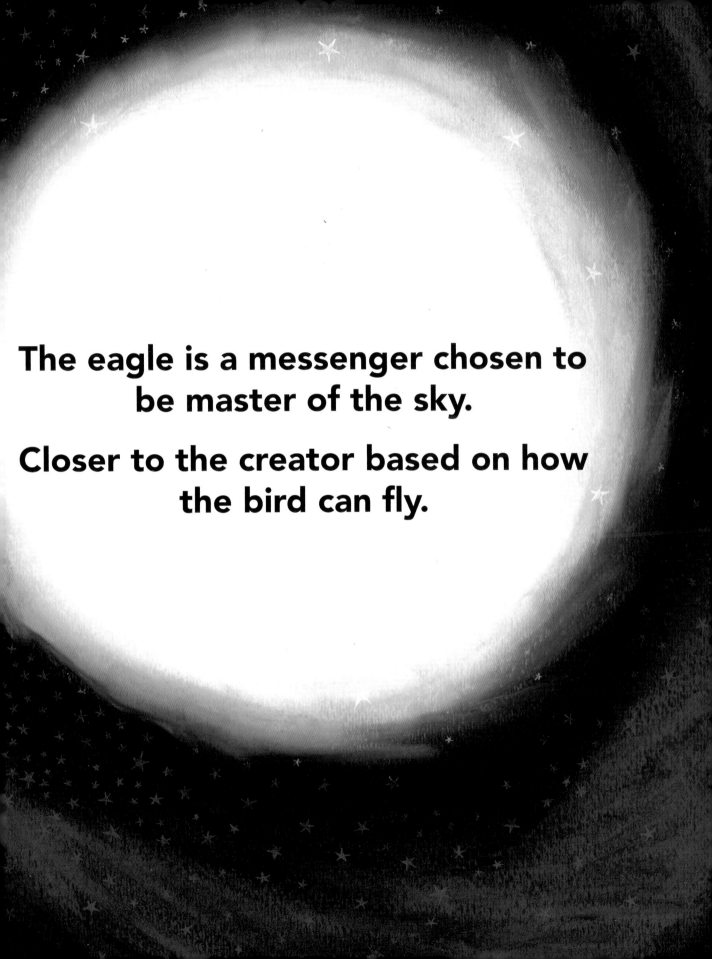

The eagle is a messenger chosen to be master of the sky.

Closer to the creator based on how the bird can fly.

F is for Feathers.

Feathers are used to decorate and tell the wearer's story.

Sometimes it tells of tragedy, sometimes it tells of glory.

G

is for Ghost.

Tribes have different views of ancestor spirits as ghosts.

Some think they were owls or other animal hosts.

Dressed or raw, an animal skin is used in many ways.

For shelter, bowls, or clothing, hides are used throughout the days.

 **is for Indigenous.**

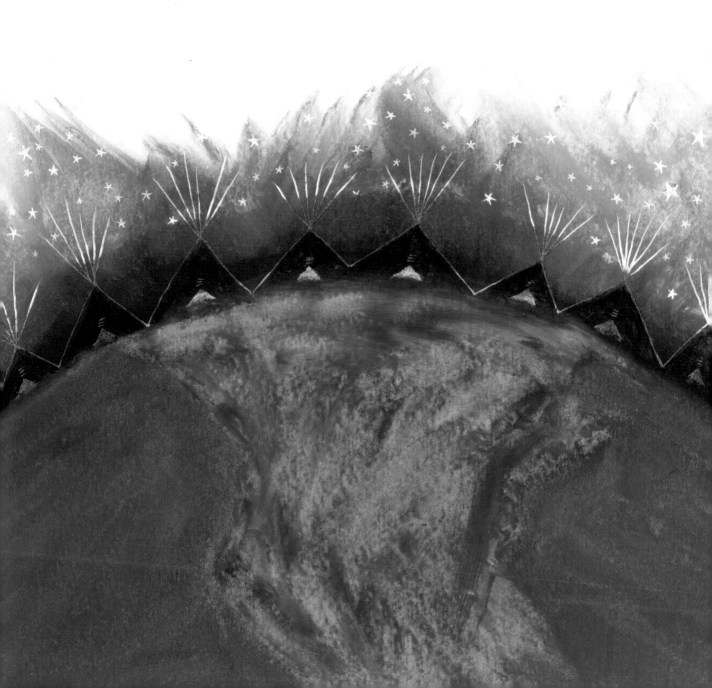

**Indigenous means native—
the first people to ever stand**

**On the earth where they make their
homes and promise to protect the land.**

J is for Jewelry.

Different tribes wear different jewelry to make themselves look good.

They craft items that they wear from gold and bone and wood.

K is for Knife.

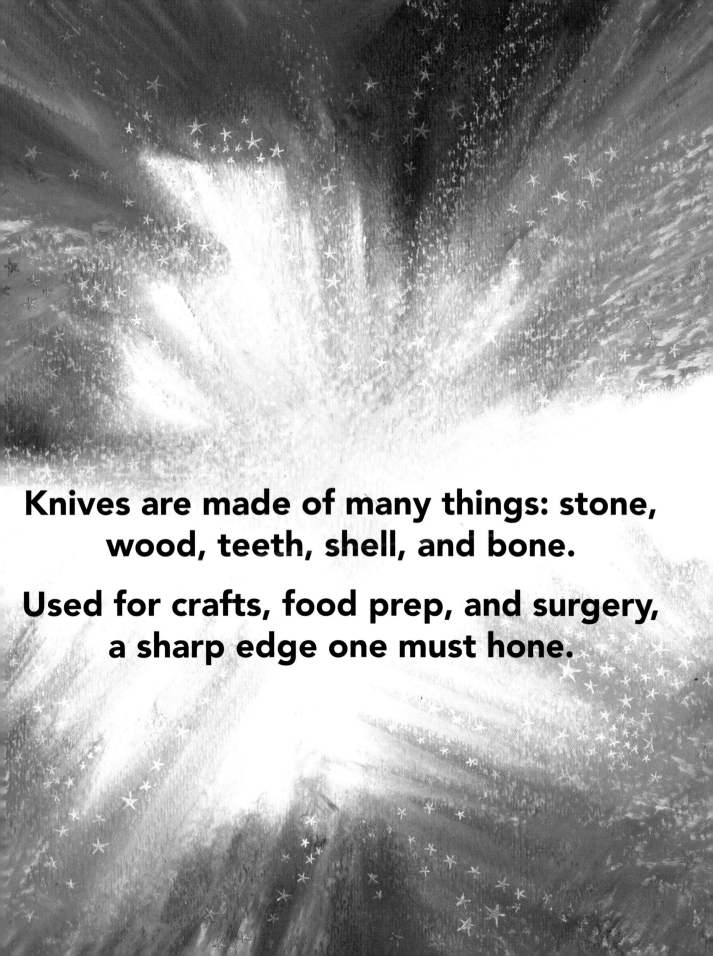

Knives are made of many things: stone, wood, teeth, shell, and bone.

Used for crafts, food prep, and surgery, a sharp edge one must hone.

L is for Lacrosse.

A sport invented by native people and still widespread today.

You use sticks with long handles and a ball to play.

 **is for Malamute.**

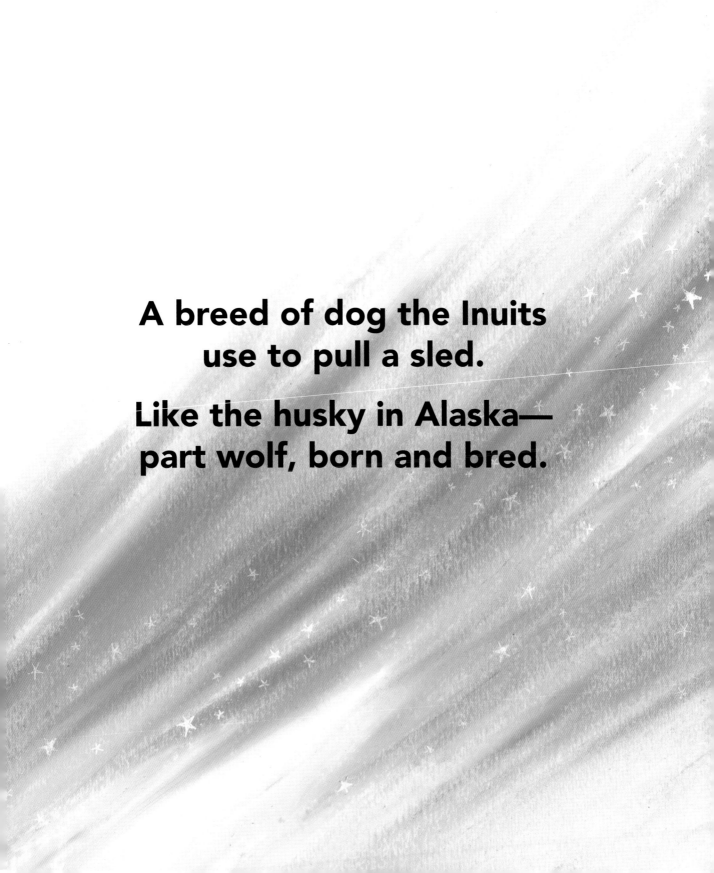

A breed of dog the Inuits
use to pull a sled.

Like the husky in Alaska—
part wolf, born and bred.

N is for Naming Ceremony.

Different tribes have different ways to give a person a name.

Sometimes elders make the call based on skills or looks or fame.

**O** is for Ocher.

A variety of natural earth oxides of iron, sand, or clay.

Some are red or yellow and used for clothing, art, or play.

P is for Pow Wow.

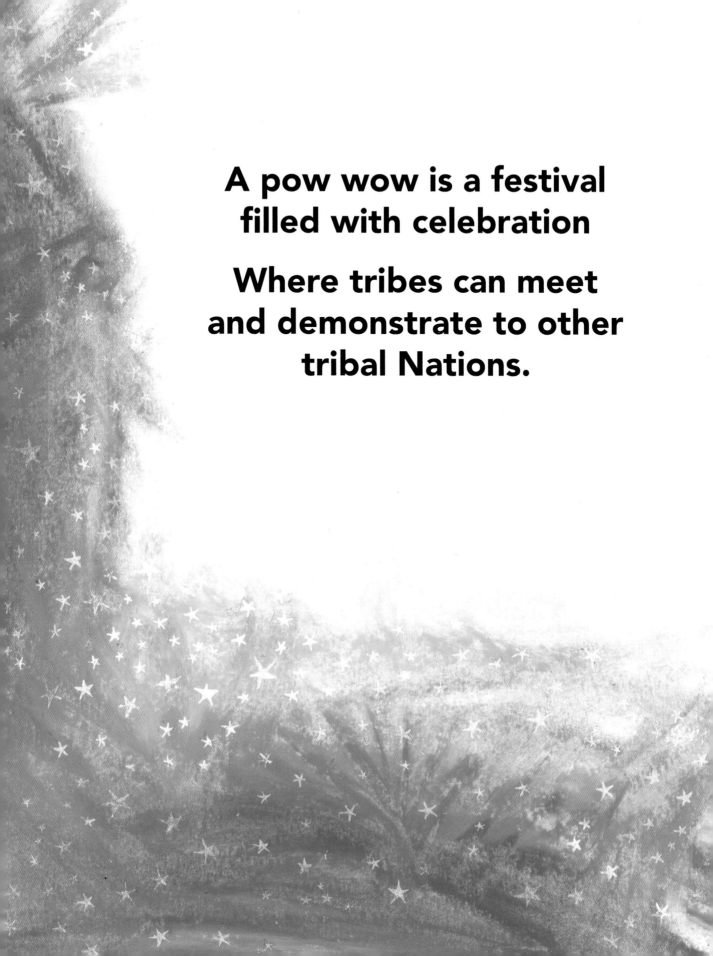

A pow wow is a festival
filled with celebration

Where tribes can meet
and demonstrate to other
tribal Nations.

Q is for Quarry.

An open pit in the earth filled with workable stone.

Native Americans make tools from a source other than bone.

 **is for Racing.**

Native Americans have enjoyed racing
on horse and on foot.

Sometimes tribes use races to help
their crops take root.

 **is for Sachem.**

A sachem is a leader,
designated chief of all.

Where a number of tribes are allies,
one man answers the call.

T is for Tipi
(also spelled Tee Pee).

A tipi is a triangular house made of animal skin

That you can move and store things in.

U is for Urn.

A vessel used in burial to shelter the remains.

Loved ones who have passed away, this pottery contains.

V is for Vision Quest.

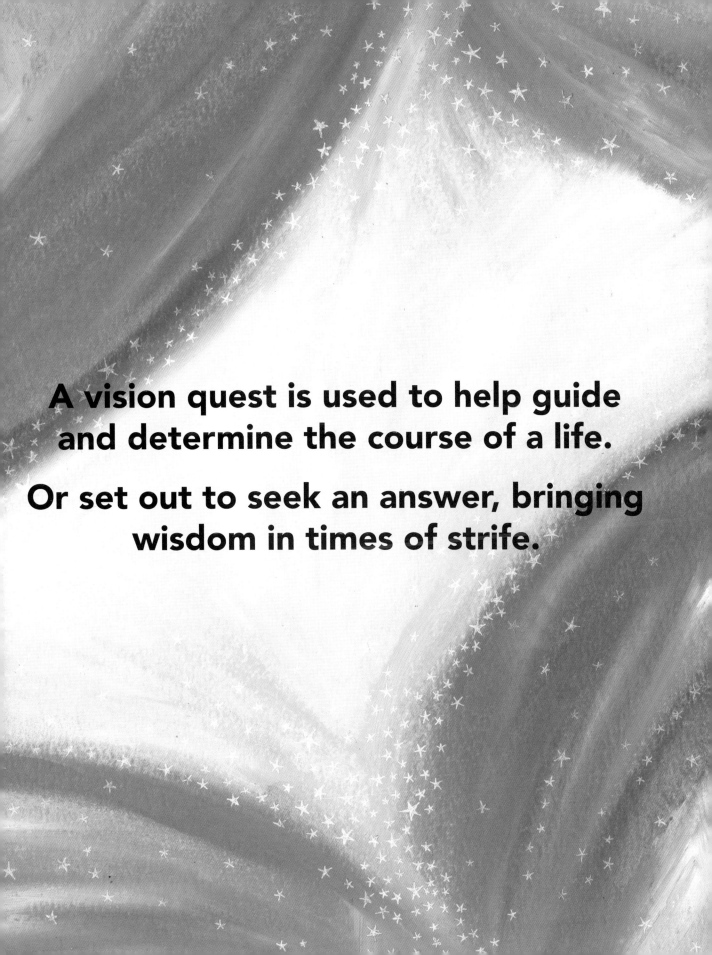

A vision quest is used to help guide and determine the course of a life.

Or set out to seek an answer, bringing wisdom in times of strife.

W is for Wampum.

Taken from the native word that means "white strings of beads,"

Wampum was just like money used for treaties, gifts, and needs.

X is for Xolotl.

Xolotl is the Aztec god of lightning,
lord of the evening star.

He pushes the sun toward the ocean
and journeys overnight with her far.

Y is for Yukon.

From a native word meaning "wide water," it makes the longest run.

Through the state of Alaska, it's a river for fishing and fun.

Z is for Zuni.

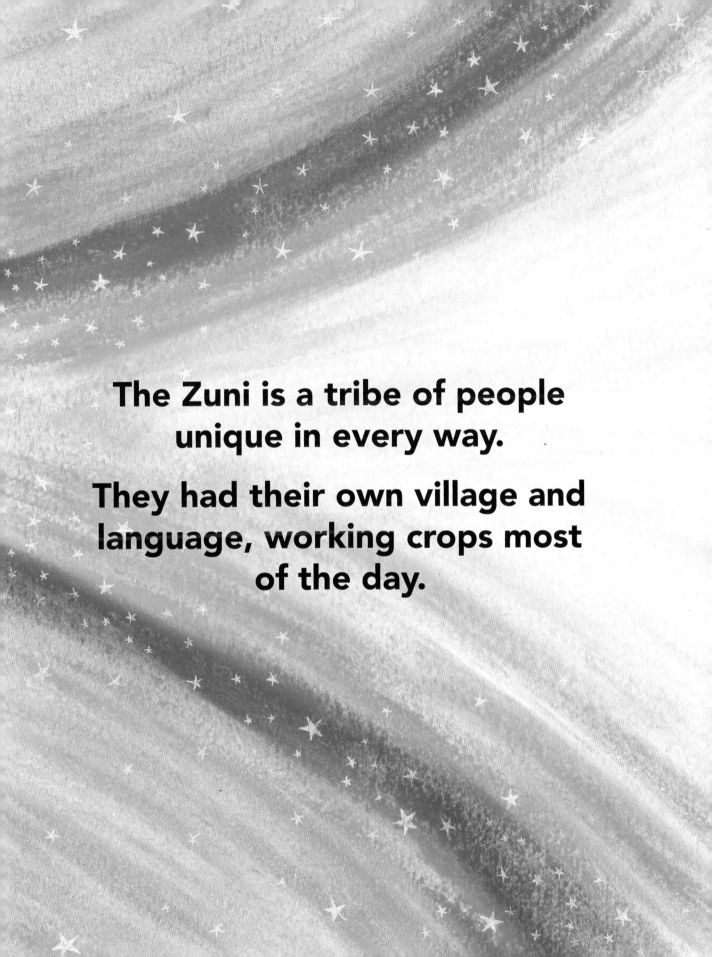

The Zuni is a tribe of people unique in every way.

They had their own village and language, working crops most of the day.

About the Authors

Colten Lechowicz is 50% Native American. He is a member of the Bois Forte Tribe, a band of the Chippewa, and is also part Lakota Sioux. Colten has lived with Grandma Lisa for most of his 11 years. To enhance Colten's reading ability and introduce him to the native culture, Colten and Grandma Lisa wrote this book. Together, they selected the words to use for each letter and Grandma Lisa created a rhyme to reinforce the learning of the subject and the reading concepts. Colten loves to play video games, has a wonderful sense of humor, and loves animals. Colten and Grandma Lisa love to travel and hope to write more books about the native culture and their adventures together.

ABOUT THE ILLUSTRATOR

Wade Patton is an enrolled member of the Oglala Sioux Tribe and was born on the Pine Ridge Indian Reservation in South Dakota. He loves the plains and the Black Hills, which feature prominently in his artwork. He currently creates his art from his studio at Racing Magpie and lives in Rapid City.

Have a book idea?
Contact us at:

info@mascotbooks.com | www.mascotbooks.com